CONTENTS

Return to the Comeraghs	9
A Walk in the Woods	10
Heritage	11
These are My People	12
Persephone on Our Street	13
The Third Winter	14
Winterscape	15
Dusk	16
The Meadow in Winter	17
We Battled Corporate Profit	18
Here Maps are Useless	19
Stain Removal	20
Imbolc	21
Funeral Haiku	22
Blindly	24
Tale of Our Times	26
First Love	27

To My Thirties, and a Certain WWOOFer	28
To a Veteran Agitator Met in a Bar	29
White Van Man	31
My Neighbour's Eucalyptus	33
Torn Stem	34
Beech Tree After Rain	35
All Morning	36
Because I listened	37
If the Climate Comes Right	38
Six Senses	40
Waking at Night as a Vixen	41
Scare	43
Poem Cat Imagined on Mishearing Lines by Madge Herron	45
Ways of Seeing the Moon	46
The Caged Bird	47
Skin	48

I Don't Do Well in the Sun Like Lily	50
Rescue	51
Childhood Sin	52
Sevenling He is Ruled…	53
Small Histories	54
Sidelong Glance	56
Bucket List	57
Meanwhile…	58
Grá: Irish for Love	60
Christening Party at Creevy Pier	61
Rebirth of a Sceptic	62
Stella	63
White Noise	65
November Haiku	66
Achill Daybreak	67
News of Weather	68
Learnings	69

Shadows of Ideas	71
More Questions that Keep Me Awake	72
We are Ocean	73
Somniloquy at Naylor's Cove	74
Spindrift	75
North Beach	76
Meditation	77
Acknowledgements	78
About the Author	79

for my family
in appreciation for their support and encouragement

Return to the Comeraghs

My feet know the contours
of this one good place.
Here strangers

look clear in my eye,
their question gentle,
Tell me, who belongs to you?

Who are your people?
When I give my townland,
my family name, they nod,

know the bones of me,
the way a fist-size rock
holds all there is to know
of the mother-mountain.

A Walk in the Woods

I glimpse a sun-glint
on what might be a coin,
pry this steel cylinder
from among fallen leaves,

read 'Winchester .243'
on the rim, trace
a finger along the steel,
feel how smooth,
designed to drive a hot projectile
through meat and bone.

A soft breath blown
across its empty neck
raises the high-pitched whistle
of a sika deer.

It wakes my inner ear
to the gun's report,
my mind's eye sees bone shatter,
knees buckle and fold,
eyelight quench
as a deer heart pumps
hot blood into forest loam.

I stand in a hunter's footprints,
scan shadows
spreading between trees.

I pocket as souvenir
the deer's voice
trapped in steel
as the sun goes down.

Heritage

Children kick through fairy fog
where summer sun burns off the dew,
reminding me of a long-gone field
hand-sown with *Fescue, Cocksfoot,
Timothy, Rye, Common Bent, Foxtail,*
dry-mixed in a galvanised bucket,
as a home baker combines
wholemeal, sifted white, oatmeal,
salt and soda to her secret recipe.

Each field, broadcast, trodden and rolled
differed from the neighbour's as each
farmwife's loaf had its own texture and savour.
Meadow and loaf held their secrets close: ratio,
number of handfuls, size of measuring hand.
The meadow was once a speckled tweed
of purples, yellows, greens and blues,
good grazing for ancient cattle breeds,
Droimeann, Kerry, Dexter and Moiled Polly,
pedigrees stretching back to the *Bó Cúailgne.*

The baker brings forth her perfect loaf
of close-grained wholemeal bread
slathered with butter to nourish
grandchildren tumbling through fairy fog.

And what will these children remember?
Only the fog, the bread, their excited running?
Or Grandmother's talk of *Daisy, Self-Heal,
Lady's Smock, Clover, Meadowsweet,
Sorrel, Yarrow,* the vanished pink smoke
of flowering grasses?

These are My People

This rock is the mountain's bone,
the mountain that carries the river
that tumbles stone to the distant ocean.
My bones sing with the cadence of water,
the mineral sparkle of rock.

A trodden path guides me towards woods
where pine martens prowl,
red squirrels strip pine cones.
Gulls forage in a plough-pleated field,
reminder of the ocean just beyond sight.
A heron stalks trout in the stream.

Nightfall. Rabbit and hare retreat
from the hunting fox. I start
at the vixen's shriek, leave the dark
to the trees, to flickering moths,
roosting blackbirds and munching slugs.

Even without a name, or inkling
of where my roots lie,
I would know this place.
Let me be blackbird, squirrel,
heron and fish, river, rock and night-fox.
These are my people.

Persephone on Our Street

From my window
there is nothing much to see.

A suburban street.

A man wearing ear protectors
trims a hedge.

Cars trundle past.
A cyclist stops
to read a text on his mobile phone.

A young woman zig-zags
between footpath and cycle lane.

As she passes, she lays her palm
on each carbuncled tree trunk.

Green sap rises
through gnarly twigs to leafbuds.

Spring is here.

The Third Winter

Earthworms freeze in dank soil,
slugs slither down, layer by layer,
closer to Hades' fire. They gleam,
pallid globules on the roots
of the pomegranate tree.
Only the dream sustains me:

Demeter unwraps two straw-wound
wine apples. Ember-lit on her palms,
they shine, red-streaked lanterns.
She saves me the choicest, as if
even now I might lean into her flank,
lay my head in her lap as her blade
splits the fruit, explores the folds
of its juice-swollen womb.
She flicks bloodripe droplets
into the pink cave of my mouth
with a halfmoon thumbnail.
I crush them one by one between
teeth and tongue, release wine-juice
in exquisite increments.

Earth Mother, all winter I yearn
for sap-rise, to walk with you
through pomegranate fields,
ripening the glistening fruit.
Your mourning overwhelms me.
I stretch my dazed mouth
for a wine-rich seed, taste
slug, bitter as cloudberry.
This is our third winter sundered.

Winterscape

rain blackens soil
worms burrow deep
blackthorns cage leaf-drift

a pale waxed disc
seals sloe jam in jars —
daylight moon

nightlong rain crawls
down the window
in its own wake

in the doe's belly
her wombfed faun's
first leap

Dusk

Fuchsia bells drip nectar,
bees fly hiveward in thinned light.

Bats in meagre skies
hoover up moths and midges.

I remember bright buttercup, dandelion,
cuckoo pint, sweet clover, vetch and trefoil;
poppy and rosebay willow for mellow mood.

This was my favourite field.
And now?

Rooks tear out divots, feast on leatherjackets.
Pheasants roost in alder, above nightfox reach.
Hedgehogs crunch snails by the compost heap.
The ride-on mower tames wild grasses to lawn.
A John Deere rumbles past, scalping August hedges.
Lights startle small birds into song.

Snarls of motorway traffic trouble the dusk.
A hidden landfill reeks of decay.

Outside of memory,
can the meadow survive?

The Meadow in Winter

sleeps under a blanket of cold.
A ball of wrens huddle in a branch-fork,
taking turns in the cosy core.

A bird-cherry in the hedge lets her last leaf go.
Buds sheathed against frost-sting,
she flaunts thoughts of blossomy fronds
against tender spring green.

Frogs sunk deep in pond mud
hold hoarse mating songs in throats
that blow bubbles to break still water,
betraying their hiding place.

Under the bird feeder, seeds dream
wheat spears in fissures,
sparrow-shelled sunflower hearts
nudge into frozen ground.

Fieldmice tunnel under tussocks;
they shape secret grass nests,
planning early litters
of pink, hairless mouselets.

Winter is the meadow's dreamtime,
the place where she sleeps herself awake.

We Battled Corporate Profit

When the future is here,
say we let maverick seed blow in
from the countryside,
let the lawn grow, dandelion suns
stud the garden, feeding early bees.

And daisies!
Long chains threaded among cuckoo-pint,
clover and meadowsweet.
Tell how we countered Big Pharma
with feverfew and self-heal.

Say we foraged for vetch, sorrel
and juicy hawthorn leaves.
Tell how we fermented wine
from sloe and wild cherry,
toasted success with elderflower champagne.

We grew stonefruit and berries,
made sure the birds got their share,
and their share of insects
and worms fattened
on lush homegrown leaves, pesticide-free.

Tell how we followed guidelines,
turned the thermostat down,
cut our air miles to zero,
took to the cycle lanes, wrapped warm
in patched, pre-owned clothes.

When the future comes,
say we battled corporate profit,
championed old, tried-and-true ways.
Tell Earth, though seas rise and she's burning,
we go on. We swear we will save her.

Here Maps are Useless

Forget cartography, calculate instead
the weight of light,

the heat of burnt-out stars,
the heft of time,

the space between love
and its perception.

Night stills the trees,
the ocean quivers, waits

for the river's penetration.
Down by the lake

signposts written in fog
dissolve memory.

Silence assembles, snags
on a place outside experience.

Stain Removal

After the war we erased the old names,
replaced the signs that showed where
ordinary people had plied their trades.
Cooks Lane, Oven Lane, Butcher's Row
the New Order transformed to honour
themselves: Convent Avenue, Marian Park,
Bishop's Street, Presbytery Drive.
                                            We knew
what we knew, but buried it deep, spoke
only in euphemism. 'She's away, her aunt
got her a job in England', we said
of an inconvenient daughter we sold
into slavery, sentenced to hard labour
where she served jailers armed with rosaries
and scissors who stole her name, then her hair,
then her child.
                            While she purged stains,
respectable ladies embroidered a new name
in a layette, monogrammed
men's shirts, snipped the last thread,
sent the washing out to the Magdalenes.

Imbolc

Today, wind plays havoc with crows,
snarls in the tall trees,
combs wintry grass into furrows.

First day of Spring, Feast of St Brigid.
What can I say of this Triple Goddess,
Healer, accidental Bishop, Saint, Keeper of Flame,

patron of blacksmiths and poets?
All this you know; and besides,
that she won by her own quick wit

and a single throw of her broad cloak
all the rich land of Kildare, where
she gathered a band of free-thinking women,

who spurned wedlock and championed
God and the poor. Christian midwives,
they ushered loved infants into the light

and stilled unwelcome wee mites
by laying-on hands in the holy name
of their Lord, Lamb of God.

See how the wind has warmed, a scent
of woodsmoke drifts from a chimney
where a farmhouse glows in dusky light?

Three ewes huddle in a corner of the field,
each with three lambs *imbolc*,
too many in belly for a two-teat ewe to rear.

On this her day, let us pray to Holy Brigid,
Goddess and Mother of the Gael, kindly
to ease the lambing and magic one lamb away.

Funeral Haiku

snow light —
buffeted seagulls settle
on red roofs

*

I smooth a sea-pebble
in my black coat pocket —
funeral offering

*

her ashes in his arms,
the widower walks
behind the empty hearse

*

sounds of three continents
fill the ancient chapel…
the organist improvises

*

admiring the hats
while the priest drones on —
cloche, kippah, ushanka

*

Jackdaws chatter by the grave
where we last met...
the same birds?

*

I drop the worry stone
among jagged marble chips —
deserted friary

*

leaving the graveyard
under the church gable
broken nest

Blindly

It is only with the heart that we can see rightly, as the essence of things is not visible to the eye. — Antoine de Saint-Exupéry, *Le Petit Prince*

We place our fingerpads over the sockets
and find not moist, flinching eyeballs
but something softer, less moulded
to contours extending around the head's
tropic of cancer: a night maker,
stealing our light.

Running our fingers over its pile,
it feline silkiness, we picture
short fur, moleskin, mousepelt;
sight jumps into our fingertips,
reads texture and darkness
hidden in unfathomable folds,
cause and effect.

&

Tracing the braille map, our fingers
cannot imagine how the terrain
might touch the soles of our feet,
what rock might trip us on our way,
or how it bubbled up from the earth's core,
molten, then cooled to an endoskeleton
to hold up all we know of the path,
even the obstacles over which we stumble.

&

In the care home the old sailor
blinded by cataracts hovers a silvery hand
over two notebooks to tell red from green:
one warm as skin under tropical sun, the other
cool as spring grass after rain.

&

The bound prisoner explores
the darkness inside the hood
with his facial nerves: the hood is black,
double-skinned against his cheeks;
its weave oozes another's coarse fear
into his nostrils and he knows the hood
is not made with cotton or hate,
but with indifference; and he is afraid.

Tale of Our Times

The children are silent in their cages,
their tears turn to sand in Arizona,
they turn small faces to the concrete floor.
They lose their mother tongue, word by word,
the littlest ones lose Mama's face, Papa
is a hollow place where a heart once glowed.

'Fake news!' cries the villain who holds the key,
'I, Leader of the Free World, decree: enemies
have no rights to children or to dreams. They come
to steal from real American children. Drive adults
back where they came from, lock children in cages.
Show them the American way.'

The children in cages yearn through endless nights
and days, no mama prepares their unhappy meals,
time erases cradle words, smiles decay, hearts ache
for *Mama, Papa*. Only armed *chupacabra* guards
come, following orders, where caged children wait
for Mama to sift the sands of Arizona tracking their tears.

Two hungers gnaw the children in their cages:
no loving hand stirs dinner on the stove,
no one cools each spoonful with her breath,
no one cares if small tongues blister;
they starve for the warm smell of Mother's hair,
for Papa to lift them, laughing, into the air.

First Love

Two heads
incline
in wordless
tête-à-tête

X-locked
arms
behind
identical
logoed backs
Gap & Gap

say this love
can't last

To My Thirties, and a Certain WWOOFer

Oh year of my thirtieth birthday,
if I'd known I would never feel older,
or that organic gardening would lose
its mud-under-the-fingernails glamour,
I'd have paid more heed
to that young man of twenty
who offered to do my spring sowing
in exchange for bed and board.
Oh thirtieth birthday, the swing
of his Blackwatch kilt fanned the silky
backs of his knees, but I feared
he'd be gone when his seed
sprouted its first leaves, and insisted
my garden didn't need his green-
fingered tending. I was wrong.

WWOOFer: International volunteer exchange on sustainable and organic farms and properties.

To a Veteran Agitator Met in a Bar

So much depends on ships going bump in the night —
ours never did, till tonight in a mid-town bar.
You hit on a girl half your age. A lost cause;
she walked off, bored, while you droned.
She'd never heard of Che, and your campaign
was aimed at her Hot Chick logoed chest. It failed,

so you turned to me. We reminisced about old, failed
campaigns, recalled the zeal of nights
spent talking politics in smoky bedsits in a one-bar
electric glow, Che on the wall, the current cause.
We thought we counted then; we were drones,
mere fodder for the latest big campaign.

Our paths didn't cross on those marches to campaign
for civil rights. You declared for war, when it failed,
you printed *Brits Out!* fliers late at night,
high on passion, coffee and Marathon bars.
I hung back when your lot burned the embassy, because
I was afraid of militants, a baton charge, the drone

of army choppers overhead. We must have seemed drone
ants to the gunner dropping teargas on campaigners
chanting *Viva Allende!* on the Ramblas. We failed
to find each other there, though we came close the night
I hid in Mercat de Sant Josep; you, nearby in a bar
while outside the Guardia cracked skulls without cause.

Days after, we caught separate trains for home because
the graduate factory's offers came, and parents droned
that it was time to earn our degrees. So we campaigned
on campus for El Salvador and student rights, and failed
to meet. We waved *Free Speech* placards when the nightly
TV news gagged dissidents, while behind bars,

the Long Kesh hunger strikers raised the bar
and starved for five demands, another hopeless cause.
Remember Thatcher's effigy in flames, the drone
of squad cars circling our parade? After, each campaign
we marched for had lost heart, and failed;
our silent candles never did *Reclaim the Night*!

We ran aground tonight in a Dublin bar, droned a while
about our old campaigns. Imagine if we'd met before
we tried to change the world, and failed. And failed.

White Van Man

Eve dreamed of faulty plumbing and exotic fruit
and woke beside a plumber in a strange hotel —
a white van man. And it was love.

He found a house for them, a fixer-upper,
she saw the sorry shell of brick and stone
and dreamed of decent plumbing and exotic fruit.

He demolished lath-and-plaster ceilings,
replaced the soffit, laid new hardwood floors,
her white van man. That, too, was love.

He gave her gleaming runs of copper piping,
brass olives, spanners, blanking caps.
He promised expert plumbing and exotic fruit,

waste traps, mixing valves and ball-cocks,
elbow bends, straight couplings and pipe dope,
her white van man. That, too, was love.

On summer nights he joined the stars in constellations
with bent connectors and compression joints,
filled her dreams with astral plumbing and erotic fruit,
her white van man. That, too was love.

Eve boasted of his expert plumbing and exotic fruit,
she spread his reputation wide by word of mouth,
her white van man. And that was love.

He worked on complicated jobs in distant counties
and slept in his workshop-van among the tools
while Eve dreamed of erotic plumbing and exotic fruit,

and though he froze all week installing solar panels,
on Sundays, by the laws of thermodynamics,
Eve warmed her white van man with ardent love.

She looked forward to their weekends of aqueous logic.
While he set her thermostat quite high with pomegranates,
she kept secret her corroding plumbing and necrotic fruit,

hummed tunes he played on a copper-pipe marimba,
inhaled his heady blend of plumbing mixed with sweat,
her white van man who smelled of love.

He drove his van down summer lanes one stripey Sunday
with Eve who saw dark spaces grow between the stars
while her secret plumbing grew narcotic fruit,
so he helped her switch her mains off. That, too, was love.

My Neighbour's Eucalyptus

With leaves shaped like swords
our eucalypt orchestra
carved surf-songs from sea air,
our neighbourhood's wind-honed
ambient music.

People complained,
the council decreed danger
to bricks and mortar,
said roots could push into drains,
rupture foundations.

Lumberjacks' saws moaned
through two spotlit nights
from a crane on a flat-bed.
Now traffic drones
where winds played unchained.

When insomnia plagues my nights,
I tune out the urban noise
of engines that startle and grind,
conjure the murdered tree, invite
its lullaby in, leaf by silvered leaf.

Torn Stem

Each branchlet
replicates
the parent plant,

each leaf dictates
the lime green shade
of its subordinates

whose edges are inlaid
in carmine,
as if human blood

flows through its veins,
the weeding hand
might feel Herb Robert's pain.

Beech Tree After Rain

The tree goes on dripping,
dripping until the sun appears
to hush the perking leaves
that listen, listen
to all the summer sounds;
birdsong, windsong, rainsong,
the quiet hum of trees.

All Morning

I've been watching
sparrows driving blue tits
from the feeder.

A collared dove swings it
like a pendulum, spilling seed
for darting mice to nibble.

Magpies mob a stalking cat
and while they chase him,
a moulting blackbird

bare-breasted
in this raw, inclement summer,
takes his chance.

I am trying to be grateful
for his skinny, bald survival,
grateful for his bright yellow

beak that lights the drizzle,
grateful for the starlings
dripping on the clothesline.

This July, more rain has fallen
than in any other summer
but I'm trying to be grateful

for this simple gift
of songbirds flying free
around birdseed in mesh cages.

Because I listened

when the music stopped,
I heard the rain snake
down the window pane
and looked beyond
to where heavy drops
beat ivy almost flat
against the dripping wall,
so heard the blackbird's
warning call and
glimpsed her
clap rain
off drenched wings
and fold them flat,
then shuffle, furtive,
into a leafy cave
she must have hollowed
underneath the vines
to hide her nesting site.
While I was tuning out
Rodrigo's liquid strings,
half-focussed on trivia
on my screen, what else
must I have missed?

If the Climate Comes Right

I.

This abundance of Devil's Glen trees
tumbles down the ravine,
crowns rake the storm with a riverine crash.

Seedpods, ash keys, sycamore wings,
seedlings in acorn cups swirl down
to wait for squirrel or bird

or boot-cleat to carry them clear.
These hedgehog-spined burrs
will grow to a sweet chestnut grove

to yield twenty years hence,
if the soil gets a good snap of frost,
if it doesn't heat up too early in spring,

if a flood doesn't sweep the topsoil away,
if crop spray doesn't drift on the wind,
if the white catkins bloom,

if bees swarm to the pollen-rich flowers,
if the seas don't encroach,
if the climate comes right.

II.

Screens show us forests on fire,
a beach cut off by barbed wire,
landfill leaching into the bay.

Jettisoned nets tangle gullbone,
shed feathers, seal-skull, rope, fish-kill,
bleached wrack, driftwood, seaglass.

A fin whale blunders upriver to die,
a storm-addled seal hauls out
and births a white pup

on the urban foreshore.
We admire the wee creature —
such sorrowful eyes — deplore

the unseasonal weather, unaware
that the petrol we burn
and our gas-heated homes cause change

that can never come right.

Six Senses

Threaded through tree-tops in the hour after daybreak:
fairy fog, God's breath, devil's pipe smoke.

Scrabble of dry leaves blowing across concrete
in this desiccating July breeze.

Deep inhalations of sunbaked meadow grasses
conjure childhood summers hay-making.

A devil's coach horse races along a bare arm,
unfazed by freckles or follicles.

Samphire needles, estuarine salt-spicules
tease the sharp edges of the tongue.

Electric currents standing the hackles on end
alert the shrew to buzzard-strike.

Waking at Night as a Vixen

The harriers crowding too close
wear the faces of strangers.
They have crossed a vast meadow
to the shelter of pines
where a woman is panting,
sweat-soaked, lungs screaming.
Pursuers in ratcatchers stalk
deep shadow, listening
for a betraying whimper.

Then relief: it was a dream on the cusp
of nightmare. Awake or almost,
untethered in a strange space
you reach for a light-switch. Not there.
An echo of baying judders your spine.
That tremor is fear, your own
and that of the dreamwoman
holding her breath, blood drumming,
curled tight, gone to ground.

You scent hounds scenting fox stink,
tracking you, or the woman. Red dots
swim into your sight: refracting eyes,
or pinprick standby light for a TV
in the room where you might be.

And the woman whose blood
was set to be spilled like secrets,
who was almost caught by the chasers,
also almost escaped when you woke
or dreamed that you woke.

You swallow a great gulp
of secrets and know

you yourself are the woman
whose bone is vixen; hunter;
foxhound and also the dreamer
trapped at dawn in your den
under the duvet, reeking of fear.

Scare

Muttered words
as the clock
strikes bedtime, 'Just

going outside
to check on the stock
before turning in'.

A to-and-fro
shuffle on gravel,
a shadow-flit,

cigarette-tip's
red predator eye
under the pear tree,

a cough
in the thickening
night

while we undress,
alive to the backlit effect
of the ceiling light,

to the eye
at the curtain-chink
we tug and pin,

locking the outside in
where the dark flaps
like crows. We brush

sparks from our hair,
nails scratch glass,
wallpaper roses stare,

the Scare sucks air
from our lungs
until there is

nothing but fear.

Poem Cat Imagined on Mishearing Lines by Madge Herron

A cat is as cruel as a tiger, Madge says.
And what is a cat, but a pint-sized tiger,
its cruelties sheathed in silken fur,
fur you could wear if not for its skimpy size.
Cat knows, and knows besides
that the wearer would be vilified, egged,
paint-daubed, possibly stoned for such attire.
Cat's eye is the eye of a storm, an emerald eye,
unlike a buzzard's that shines with green spite,
or the robin's berry-eye, all 'Rest ye merry'
subterfuge, a bonhomie that any small bird
could tell you masks a vicious streak.
Cat has been shocked to see Robin in rage drill
through a songbird's skull. The murderer!
Cat, for all his tiger stealth and cruelty
would never do that *to let the music out.*

Ways of Seeing the Moon

As cross-sawn pine trunk,
as a lantern caught in a tree-fork,

as many-eyed lumpen potato,
as leery man-at-the-window,

as new-minted coin,
as mystery, mirror, spy,

as shadowed colony,
as a porthole on night,

as blackness, as an act of faith,
as new and invisible,

as darklight,
as cold shadow-caster,

as magnet,
as midwife of tides,

as once-in-a-season blue,
as goddess in her maiden phase,

as blood-sister, rocker of cradles,
as a drowned face in a well,

as split-lipped hare,
as night-lit sky-mushroom,

as ghost of the sun,
as the gleam in the wolf's eye,

as untethered balloon,
as Moon.

The Caged Bird
after Gerald Dillon

She carries me into the street, settles us
under the mural the Council commissioned
some out-of-work vandals to paint:
components of lightness; wings, pillows,
feathers, a contrail, mackerel clouds.
None of it's real, just paint on a wall,
not a sky I could fly. Nobody speaks
to one with despair in her eyes.
She hopes I'll stay bound
in this sparrow-size cage,
but my wings poke through the wires.
I'm her crow; where she goes, I go.
She is me, I am she. If I could, I'd fly
into the painted sky, set us both free.

Skin

She holds her breath,
throws wide the drapes
another's hand twitched shut,
shakes free the other's skin cells
run-and-felled from tape to hem,
hunts them along the tops of doors,
on picture rails and underneath the bed.
She damp-dusts, vacuums, disinfects:
there's always more. She lifts a rug,
the sly half-smiles of toenail tips
outwit her vacuum's crevice tool
to slip between the floorboards.

She holds her breath,
afraid to breathe shape into old fingerprints
fixed with a spiteful *haw*
on a mirror's bevelled edge,
inside a rim of crystal glass,
or tarnished to a silver serving spoon.
Comparisons odious as afterbirth
forgotten in a fridge
hang between her and the other's spawn
she must step-mother at weekends.
Sheddings from their clothes
sift through the house,
they settle white on the counter-top,
at every step the stairs hold follicles
that make her cough.

She holds her breath at Christmas,
masked against the scurf
that lurks between joists,

she hauls boxed baubles from the rafters.
The brats insist: it's what their mummy did.
Powerless against this haunting by a mortal,
her cells mutate, usurper to usurped.
Like every second wife, she holds her breath,
does what she must to hold her tenure,
weaves slut's wool into a doll
stuffed with stray eyelashes and sloughed skin,
sutures the torso with moulted hairs,
twines curly strands to bind the neck,
selects a thumbnail sliver for her scimitar.

I Don't Do Well in the Sun Like Lily

Lily with her speckled throat
and tongue made for kissing
flashed a ring her auntie stole
from Woolworths on Saturday.
She swore the stone was as real
as her glamour. She wore
a store-bought dress printed
with showy flowers, a stunner
I had to pretend to admire
and try not to gag on my envy.
I strolled through the park
at her side in my mother-
stitched button-through cotton,
Lily all fashion-plate glam, hips
swinging, an eye-catcher named,
she said, for the perfumed flower
in the formal beds.
                        A scarlet
beetle crept over my wrist,
parting the hairs in search
of something lush to munch;
a gem, polished and gleaming.
I slipped it into the bold,
open mouth of a Stargazer Lily.

Rescue

Oh for a muse of fire that would ascend
The brightest heaven of invention. — Shakespeare, *Henry V*

For me, no dead poet's lady with marbled pout,
nor calendar girl, all tits and leather.
Mine's *a muse of fire* in screaming tender,
blue lights flashing. Buff in turn-out gear,
he knuckles along smoke-filled corridors,
his hot breath at my ear ignites my tinder.
He comes my way aslant, blasts through obstacles;
he's my crosswind bringing oxygen, the draught
that fans my flicker into flame. He pours
accelerant — and I'm a conflagration.
He poses on my kitchen wall in Kevlar
and asbestos. When I'm choked in smoky dark,
cold and barely smouldering, I dial his number.
He blares his siren, fans my spark to wildfire.

Childhood Sin

…the earthworm
we split
to see the head
grow a tail
the tail
a new head

instead
five simple hearts
failed
one by one…

another regret

Sevenling: He is Ruled…

He is ruled by geometry,
stacks his books by width and height
in strict rectangular symmetry.

Theme rules my library,
Moby Dick, *The Ancient Mariner* and Jacques Cousteau
lean against *The Perfect Storm* on *The Sea, The Sea*.

Yet we are perfect bound.

Small Histories

What's not to love?
The tray saves on legwork:
it ferries washing from the line
to the airing cupboard.

Upside down, it saves the hair
from sudden downpours.

The dull patina preserves
ancient teapot rings
and watermarks.

It flips from serving-tray
to wall art in a tick
by virtue of a mounting hook
and still life *découpage*
from gallery catalogues.

Scribbled on the back
are doctors' fees in guineas,
costings for christenings
and a funeral tea,
a former owner's weekly spend
on bread, milk, tobacco,
coal and Friday fish,
a laundry list.

*1964 the 10th of June the day
my life changed forever*
is a mystery in copperplate.

Why *Morris Minor Jan '53*
we'll never know. And never
understand what prompted us
to buy, unexamined,
'Lot 105, Good Tray'.

We're glad we did; we've tied
a pencil to the handle.

Sidelong Glance

A steam-gush escapes
the boiling kettle,
purls in kitchen quiet,

twists a yarn that ties
washing-up bowl
to ceiling,

a vapour rope
the mind climbs skywards,
clear of anchored day.

Bucket List
Keep Ithaka always in your mind.   — C.P. Cavafy

I've never been to Greece and now
have little hope of getting there.
Australia, too, has been erased
from future plans, and Newfoundland,
my one-time Ithaka — first item
on my bucket list — a destination fed
on full immersion in Sunday travel
supplements and careful scrimping
day-to-day, has fallen through.
Time and age have come between
me and my plans. Whatever Ithaka I set
my heart on now, must be within
a half-day's reach by bus and train
or from the comfort of my armchair.
And yet, I cling to hope.

Meanwhile…
i.m. Porter, a.k.a. Wullemberg Count Hawk. A good dog.

Meanwhile our lives go on
much as before
but grass has grown over the path
you wore in the lawn,
magpies menace
the songbirds in the yard
without you to chase them,

next door's marmalade cat
with the fire-struck eyes
stalks the ground-feeding doves,
you don't come when I call
but the children still play
in the woods by the river
without you to chivvy them home,

they swim in the sea
without you dog-paddling
offshore as lifeguard.
Meanwhile, I chatter on
as if you were here
but you don't quirk an eyebrow
to say, Already, enough!

The door to your kennel
framed such an ache
that we took it apart
plank by plank,
we've folded away
all our dog-scented things,
the brush and stainless steel bowl,

your hair-laden Indian blanket,
the muzzle you wore in the street.
Some days I catch a black-and-tan flash
bounding over the landscape —

woodland or mountain, the field
near your grave, then memory
makes you appear in a gap between dreams.

Grá: Irish for Love
Birthday Poem for H.K.R.

Holding you in those first hours, I saw you
Open your eyes wide, as you
Listened to my familial voice. Texting friends, I
Left the auto-correct version. In three years
You have grown into it, *grá-daughter*; love made you so.

Christening Party at Creevy Pier
For Robert

The sea festooned in its froth of waves
echoed your great-grandmother's lace
that tumbled over your broderie gown
from piqué collar to where your toes
submerged in stiffened cotton.

A breeze ruffled your starched hem
and banished the wispy rain at sea,
and someone called to the children,
'A trawler, look!' Then silence,
while everyone turned just as the ocean
conjured a pod of sleek dolphins
ploughing a course for St. John's Point.

That day, we gave you a name that means
Bright, Shining, all the world at your feet,
earth, sea, air — and later, a lighthouse
to sweep your path clear
under the fire of stars.

Here is my wish for you:
may you always meet kindness,
and carry kindness enough in your heart
to douse the greed of bee-killers,
seed-stealers and plastic polluters;
may you one day pass this teeming ocean
to your own child, pristine
as great-grandmother's lace.

Rebirth of a Sceptic

I was once like you.
Warned against greed
and smoking blind
the opium of the people,
I paid no mind,
donned Gucci blinkers,
let priests and bankers lead my thinking.

They led me down a road of many turnings.
I did not turn aside,
or read the signs,
or listen when wise men from the East
and mystic women
spoke of second chances.
I was satisfied Nirvana could be bought
by small investments
from accumulated profit,
a sometime coin in a beggar's cup.

Now I hump my crooked house
one-footed in the night,
forced to eat a righteous path
and leave the essence of myself
to warn of many futures.
You who pass heedless through your human life,
heed the hieroglyphics of a humble snail
and live a joined-up life.

Stella

Our sister Stella scans the dark for crystal
stars mapped in the astronomy book
she knows by heart from start to end
and pinpoints Pegasus tethered in a stall
of woven cosmic wire
beside a pool

of stellar light no sane eye sees, but Stella spools
strung crystals
on her arms as any half-baked woman wired
to the moon from reading zodiac books
might, and stalls
her explanation till night ends,

as end
it must, then takes the pool
cue she uses to point out galaxies into the third stall
in the ladies' loo where a crystal
chandelier lights the cover of her astronomy book
inlaid with silver wire.

She channels her guide via telepathic wire —
Galileo, Galileo — from the Cosmos' invisible end
to pool
his astral knowledge with secrets in her star book
and so end
dispute, forestall

debate and stall
unscientific speculation. Galileo's haywire
answer sent by satellite, crystal
clear to Stella's stargazy mind upends
extant theory: Pegasus' bright pool
is a porthole on the Next Dimension in Stella's book.

At Trinity College Library, Stella's *Stellar Book*
is treasured like *The Book of Kells*, installed
in a pool
of fibre-optic light, alarm-wired.
Meanwhile Stella — wonders never end —
cracks codes by casting tumblestones and crystals.

Heir to his trans-stellar gene pool, high on crystal
meth, she transcribes Galileo's starlore in her book —
our Stella, wired and on her wonky orbit to the end.

White Noise

Rubber soles *creep-creep* on the corridor,
from the carpark below a car door's whump! Oh,

say we're not too late. Summoned relatives tip-toe,
their indrawn breath an *oooh*!

held long in the muffled shhh! of the sick-room,
the water cooler gurgles *water-wasser-agua-eau*.

Electronic *chirp*, *chirp* from the monitor,
the ventilator's rhythmic *Hush—O. Hush—O.*

The small hand *snip-snip-snip* scissors time. Oh,
Clock, go slow, give us one day more.

Tic   tictictic   tic. The heart cricket sings off-beat, slow
soft-pedalled flatline note: diminuendo.

Rattled beads shake out maraca prayers for the dead, Sorrowful Mysteries: *Thou, Oh Lord, shalt ope* —

Starched sheet falls with a whispery sigh over cold
stilled face, crisp as snow.

Hinges creak as a soul flies from the window.
Vigil-keepers sit. And sit. And… nothing more

till the ambulance chopper's whappa-whap, touch-and-go
heart on ice airborne, plus medico.

November Haiku

in yellow raincoat
the gardener sprays moss-kill
on winter pathways

*

blackbirds watching
the flail trimming the hedgerow —
abandoned nest

*

torrential rain
against a backdrop of yews…
pyjama Sunday

*

at the lakeside
the heron takes sudden flight…
feral mink

Achill Daybreak

Out of a cave of dreams,
the view comes clear
with brightening dawn.

Cold light lifts
lacy whitecaps
on the sea's surface,

a sloped field lists
into a hollow between hills,
sheltering long-haired sheep.

The wind combs coarse wool
backwards
against its grain,

ruffles dyed rumps;
pink, blue and violet
flag the growing light.

Among close-nibbled grasses,
rush tussocks are strings
resisting windfingers' music.

Out of the gloom
white gables gleam,
light fills an apex window.

Headlamps tug the coast road
from village to village
past rows of emptied houses,

to where the bridge at Achill Sound
spans surging seas
to leave the island.

News of Weather

Don't throw in the towel,
Michael Gallagher, postman in Ballyshannon
says the signs are good
for a nice spread of weather
from now on into winter. The stork
is on the move. Out delivering letters,
Michael watches to see where he goes.

Sheep heading for the hills
and out onto the open spaces,
heather blossoming in the Blue Stacks Mountains
and the new moon coming in
herald the summer that never got started,

yet a spokesman for Met Éireann
soothsaying under a glass
pyramid in Glasnevin
does not share his confidence.

The stork is out and Michael watches where he goes.

Meanwhile, in Sandycove,
hot dogs take to the waves.

Statues read the clouds
over Cork County Hall in stony silence.

The Goldie Fish predicts good drying
in Shandon, a three-sheet wind at least,
but keep a weather eye on the washing.

The Met. Office gets the forecast wrong, often
weather is a local issue.

Learnings

We learned fear
from the goggie-gaw
goose-stepping
the stream's edge,
ready to carry off any child
who strayed within range.

We pedalled home fast
from school, no stopping
to play or explore
the dammed swimming hole.

We believed what we were told:
that the goggie-gaw's nest
was a tangle of children's bones,
his long neck was coiled
to drive his dagger-beak
into our eyes,

eyes he would swallow
like glittering trout fished
from the shallow stream.

Years passed before wisdom
revealed that rattle of bones
was a lonely chick champing
his beak, begging for food,

the nest in the tallest tree
was an untidy heap of sticks,
the goggie-gaw a grey heron
more fearful of us than we
should have been of him,

his repute as kidnapper a ruse
to hurry us home to our chores.
Enlightened, we watched
his slow patrol, spearfishing
frogs and brickeens, learned

to be still, to mimic
the grey bird's solitude,
absorb his tenacity and patience,
make them our own.

Shadows of Ideas

Could it all be connected?

In Rome's Campo dei Fiori,
near free thinker Giordano Bruno,
condemned to burn in silence
in an iron mask,
among stalls selling aubergines,
persimmons and cheap Murano glass,
an American hawked print-outs
of Milosz's 'Campo dei Fiori', for cash.
Only one euro. Read this.

Later, at the Terrina fountain,
I read this legend on the rim:
Do good and let them talk.

Back in my hometown,
outside Campo dei Fiori Restaurant,
among the literal translations
on the menu board:
fish in a sauce of mariner; burned bones,
under one untranslatable dish: *If you know
what this means, please tell us.*

More Questions that Keep Me Awake

I asked Google, 'Do dolphins sleep?'
Google answered with a page of links
to academic sites. 'Do whales sleep?'
I asked whalefacts.org late at night.
'Yes', came the answer,
'one hemisphere of Whale's brain
sleeps, the other powers the beast,
reminds it to swim and eat,
to breach and breathe.

'What if I dream of whales?' I asked Moon.
Moon answered, 'Sometimes, a dream
is just a dream.' Then I asked Ocean,
'Do dolphins dream?' The waves whispered,
'Hush, curious human, sleep!'

We are Ocean

We are ocean, all of us. Ocean
where Salmon and Dolphin once leapt,
gulping clean air above waves that tumbled
one over another, as they should;

where Dolphin's shining teeth snatched
Salmon mid-air, muscled him down his throat,
one life giving life to another,
exchanging molecules, as they should.

How does it feel to be dead?

Living our small lives, we come to the shore.
Fearing Earth's reprisal, an exchange
of zoonotic burdens, we keep our distance
one from another. We are ocean.

Our town elders knew, added Mermaid
to our coat of arms; also Martlet, bird
without feet, condemned to endless flight
in pursuit of knowledge. Knowledge we ignore,

to our peril. There is nothing here to save us,
no Dolphin, nor Salmon; no Mermaid
nor mythic legless bird. Swallows swoop
in endless pursuit of insects,

molecules change places. Waves tumble
seaglass, grind it back to sand.
Two mallards fly past a rainbow.
The rainbow dissolves in dark cloud.

Ocean, how will it feel to be dead?

Somniloquy at Naylor's Cove

Out of sound of the town I step out of gloam
into this parallel time where ghost-bathers
pose on the Lido.

Faint voices float on air heavy with petrichor,
cargo ships slide over a grey horizon
under linen skies.

The sea beats with a whale heart, crumbles
concrete and changing huts. Wildflowers gleam
on the cliff path,

the cove cradles a Buddleia's soporific scent,
now bee-hum is silenced, early moths flicker,
portents of dusk,

a glimpse of a portal ajar on Otherwhere.
The seas made us. The body knows: blood sings
the sea's pulse,

sweat brines our skin. Our tears flow saline,
sea-minerals harden our bones, the seas moor us.
We are drawn to thin places

where hill-fog meets sea-mist, rock meets ocean.
Surrender to moon-tug, to all things that shine,
let spirit slip bone, tides claim us.

Spindrift
After Helen Quill, 3 ceramic pieces

An exhaled breath caught
on frosted blackthorn

ghost crabs on white coral sands...
a shiver caught in a sidelong glance

seventeen curved notes
nestled in a blown bird's egg —
starling song

North Beach

Gabions brace against storm, waves nibble the cliff,
leach toxins from the buried dump.

Swans meet rising seas at the harbour mouth.
White feathers rim the water's edge.

Great black-backed gulls take flight,
webbed feet drip sea-sparkle.

No one else comes here at dusk.

Clouded memories, pebble-trickle, seaglass.
Moonlight smooths troughs and peaks.

Her father's people were stone,
her mother's were seal folk.

And her child?

Born of the moon's tug and the sea's womb-water,
her child is all ocean; salt air billows her lungs.

This sea-washed space between high and low tide?
The moon's gift.

Meditation

You don't need to believe in a god to pray,
you don't need faith in a creed,
or a blue-robed virgin to intercede,
or a saint as intermediary to plead your case.
Anyone can light a candle in the gloom,
sit in a quiet place and contemplate the flame,
a flicker strives for height, blackens the wick.
Wax heats and drools, smoke curls upwards.
You don't need words.
Send your longing out into the world and wait
for the emptiness inside to be filled.
All you need do is breathe.
That too is prayer.

ACKNOWLEDGEMENTS

Many thanks to the editors of the following journals and anthologies where some of these poems were first published: *Poetry Ireland Poetry Town*, Bray Poetry Walk, Curator Jane Clarke; *Live Encounters Poetry and Writing*, ed. Mark Ulyseas; *The Weekend Magazine*; *There Will be Time*, Writing at the Coast Project, ed. Maria Isakova Bennett; *Drawn to the Light Press*, ed. Orla Fay; *Blue Pepper*; E*mpty House, Poetry and Prose on the Climate Crisis*, ed. Alice Kinsella & Nessa O'Mahony; *Boyne Berries*; *Coast to Coast to Coast*, ed. Maria Isakova Bennett; *Spontaneity*; *Dogs Singing*, ed. Jessie Lendennie: *Flare*; *The Music of What Happens*, Purple House Anthology of New Writing, ed. Tanya Farrelly; *Poets Meet Politics*, ed. Hungry Hill Writing; *Tearing Stripes off Zebras WEB Anthology*, ed. Nessa O'Mahony.

I would like to express appreciation to friends and family in Ireland, England and the USA for their encouragement and support, especially for providing a calm space in which to write.

Many thanks also to my colleagues in Hibernian Writers and in Green Kite Writers for their close reading of my poems and their invaluable suggestions.

Several poems in this collection were inspired by a residency at Tyrone Guthrie Centre, Annaghmakerrig and also at Heinrich Böll Cottage, Achill Island. I am also grateful for a bursary awarded by the Heinrich Böll Association.

BREDA WALL RYAN grew up on a farm in Co Waterford and now lives by the sea in Co Wicklow. Her poetry for the most part invokes the ocean, the natural world and a personal and ancient mythology. Her awarded fiction has appeared in *The Faber Book of Best New Irish Short Stories* and *The New Hennessy Book of Irish Fiction*. Her poetry is widely published in print and online, broadcast on community and national radio and translated into Irish and Romanian. She was selected for Poetry Ireland Introductions Series and Poetry Ireland Review's The Rising Generation. A founding member of Green Kite Writers and Hibernian Writers, she has read at poetry events throughout Ireland, the UK and also in the US. Her poetry awards include iYeats Poetry Prize, Poets Meet Painters, Dromineer Poetry Prize, Over the Edge New Writer of the Year, The Gregory O'Donoghue International Poetry Prize and the Dermot Healy International Poetry Award. *In a Hare's Eye* (Doire Press 2015) won the Shine/Strong Award for a First Collection. *Raven Mothers* followed in 2018.